The kids'
guide to
Parents

Copyright © 1982 Richard Drew Publishing Ltd.,

First Published in 1982

RICHARD DREW PUBLISHING LTD.,
20 PARK CIRCUS,
GLASGOW G3 6BE,
SCOTLAND

ISBN 0 86267 007 1

Printed in Great Britain

All royalties from the sale of this book
will be donated to
THE SAVE THE CHILDREN FUND,
Mary Datchelor House,
Grove Lane,
Camberwell,
London SE5 8RD

The kids' guide to Parents

All the cartoonists appearing in this book have given their work free of charge, so that the royalties may be donated to THE SAVE THE CHILDREN FUND

SAVE THE CHILDREN is Britain's largest international charity caring for more than half a million children in over 50 countries, and for nearly 10,000 a day in the UK. These world wide operations cost more than £20,000 a day, subscribed at home and abroad. Over the years SAVE THE CHILDREN has raised and spent nearly £80,000,000 and has brought relief, food, care and hope to millions of children.

In buying the book you are supporting many desperately needed projects in the United Kingdom and the rest of the world.

"Ever get one of those days when all your parents' opinions seem reasonable?"

"Not just now Dad – I've got a headache!"

Quanda

"He said three words today —
'hallo...hallo...hallo'!"

CHIC

9

MUST YOU TREAT ME LIKE A CHILD? ...

"Why must we always have a sensible adult at *our* parties? You and Mum never ask one to your's!"

"I just don't believe you can still hear Radio London."

"That chemistry set we bought should keep him quiet for a while."

"So much for our voluntary contribution towards school books."

"Same here . . . I just don't know what I'd have done with myself if Dad hadn't bought us the TV . . ."

"YOU SAID NOT TO WALK ACROSS YOUR CLEAN FLOOR IN MY DIRTY SHOES!"

"That's right – you can't blow it up!"

"Come in and get your tea quickly – Dad wants help with his homework."

"MY DAD ONCE HID MY POCKET MONEY UNDER THE SOAP—IT TOOK ME A WEEK TO FIND IT."

"THE LADY ON THE T·V AD ALWAYS SMILES."

22

I'VE A FEELING THIS IS IT! ...

"Same row every year – Mum wants to watch Wimbledon, Dad wants the Test."

"WE'RE NOT LETTING YOU GO AWAY
AND JOIN THE CIRCUS AND THAT'S FINAL!"

"Mine's in her second childhood too –
calls my feet tootsie-wootsies."

"My Dad's bonds have risen 20% –
I think I'll tap him up for a new bike."

"Been brainwashed! . . . That wouldn't take much water."

"What am I going to be when I pass all my exams? A pensioner I think."

"Shall I sweep what's left of our car into the garage Dad?"

"10.30, I said to her –
you can go to the
puberty initiation rites
so long as you're home
by 10.30 . . ."

"Don't tell me the white mice have escaped again!"

"We shall have to stop him watching Spider-man."

"You know it's been a great party when his parents say never again."

"Here he comes – why do we have to listen to this stuff just when we're trying to nod off?"

"No, it's not burglars, Dear, it's only Samantha looking for the chocolate biscuits!"

35

36 "How much of a mess can we make?"

37

"Well if Grandma promises not to kiss you will you come down?"

"Phew! – This jogging sure is hard work!"

COME ON, DADDY — TIME FOR
BUY - BUYS ! "

"You expect me to
eat a potato which
has two great big
appealing eyes, pleading
with me not to ?"

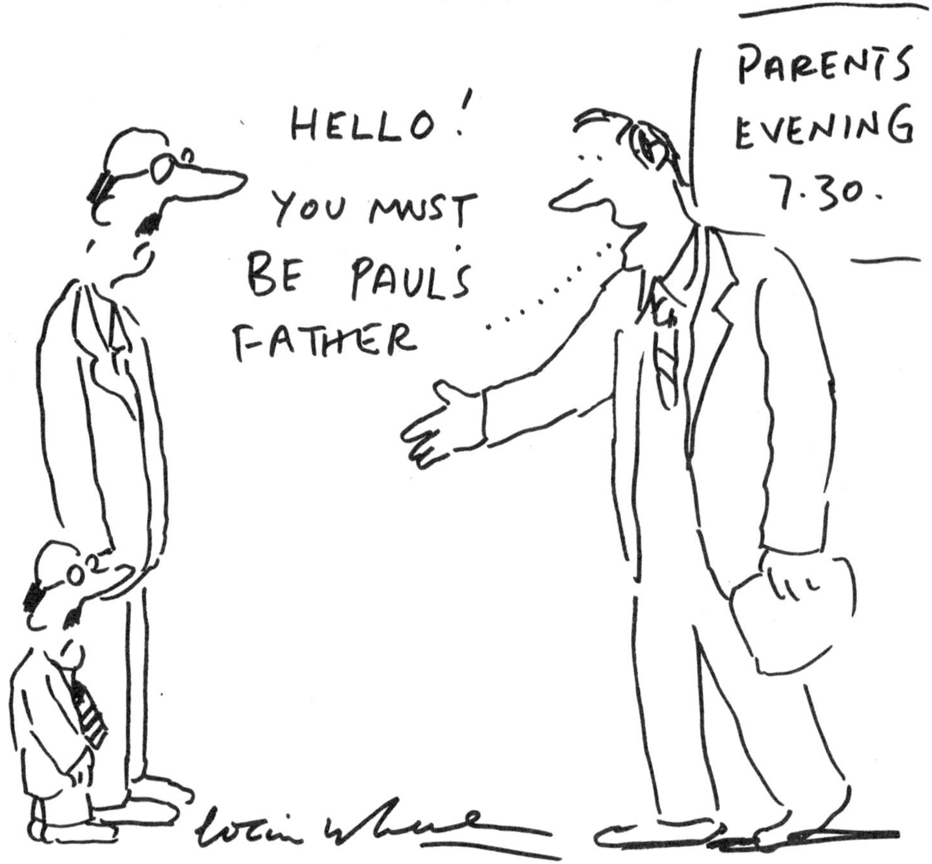
HELLO! YOU MUST BE PAUL'S FATHER
PARENTS EVENING 7·30.

"_MUST_ YOU STOP AT EVERY TREE?"

"Good job I keep my water pistol filled up! – Eh Dad!!"

"It's amazing, at home she won't wipe a cup."

"And how is our little scientist getting on with his chemistry set?"

43

YOU'RE RIGHT! BAKED BEAN AND STRAWBERRY JAM SANDWICHES ARE DELICIOUS!!

44

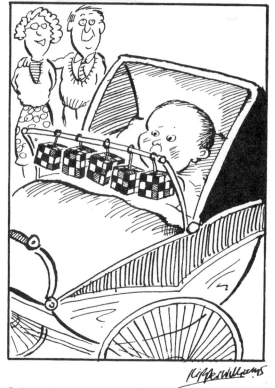

Originally printed in the
TIMES EDUCATIONAL SUPPLEMENT.

" . . . And supposing I refuse to go to jail and miss a turn?"

"You certainly can eat . . . are you being sponsored?"

"Well Nurse, it was a bit daft putting me next to this mirror!"

"No Mary, it's not what a policeman
gets for a night shift."

"Have you finished using Tiddles'
flea spray yet Mum?"

48

"But I only had a bath yesterday!"

"Hard day at school, Son?"

HI DAD! I'VE BEEN HELPING THE CHIMNEY SWEEP!

THEY NEVER GO ON LIKE THIS IN THE
TELLY COMMERCIALS!

"I do hope we're not spoiling him Sidney!"

"I PUT MUSTARD ON HIS FINGERNAILS TO STOP HIM BITING THEM!"

"Let's leave running away till tomorrow Sid – only I've got my favourite for dinner!"

I couldn't find the tea strainer, so I used the fly swatter."

"Has he shown you his new carpenter's set?"

"I know you're still only four feet tall Gary, but you'll just have to be a little patient."

"I understand that you two met in the dark."

"The picnic's off. Mum says if you know as much about fixing cars as you did about fixing the washing machine, we wouldn't get to the end of the road anyway."

" YOU COULDN'T LOOK AFTER HIM AS
   WELL, COULD YOU ? "

" DAD, IF YOU WON'T BUY ME AN ICE
  CREAM I'LL JUMP ON YOUR
  SANDCASTLE ! "

"He's a wonderful baby – we don't know we've got him."

"Ask me about sex
some other time, dear . . .
Mummy's got a headache . . ."

63

"Fetch the Sheriff, Hank, – Billy the Kid's in town!"

"They charge extra for miracles."

"Huh! – we're never going to catch any tadpoles at this rate!"

68

"Dad's okay I suppose – but he can be very childish at times."

"It should be my little girl
that you take on your knee!"

" EITHER THIS DOLL IS DEAD, OR
MY WATCH HAS STOPPED ! "

"Your father's going to kill you when he finds out that you went to the match dressed like that!"

RAG.

"Look Mum, you're not putting on weight . . . anyway I like you fat."

"In the morning we did
our ABC, and in the
afternoon we did micro-
computer programming."

73

"Barnes Wallis – I won't tell you again!"

"I like that, – it does something for your face,"

"WELL, YOU MIGHT HAVE _ASKED_ BEFORE YOU BORROWED MY DOLL'S CLOTHES!"

"WHY CAN'T HE GO OUTSIDE AND PLAY LIKE OTHER BOYS?"

NAYLOR

"If we're playing 'mothers and fathers', don't just sit there – my dollshouse needs painting!"

"Don't be silly – who ever heard of a girl being the Doctor?"

77

"I don't care how dirty they get
on the television adverts."

"I MUST BE REACHING PUBERTY I
TOOK A BATH THIS MORNING WITHOUT
BEING TOLD TO !!"

"But I don't want custody of the children."

"They're crafty y'know – they realise
we'll do the opposite to what they tell
us to do so sometimes they tell us to do
what they don't want us to do."

"What I can't understand is why my brother
has two sisters and I only have one . . ."

"I suppose having a father in the Police Force does hold certain advantages!"

"All right Paul, Miss Tibbs is here for your lessons, where have you hidden the piano?"

"It's always the same – everytime I tell him to shut up and listen to my advice based on a lifetime's experiences I realise I haven't had any."

"He's bright for his age all right – he's writing to the N.S.P.C.C."

83

"For heaven's sake get him a glass of water so we can all get some sleep!"

84

"I WOULDN'T MIND 'AVING T'WEAR
HAND ME DOWNS IF I 'AD AN OLDER
BRUVER INSTEAD OF AN OLDER SISTER."

"Uncle Bill must be coming –
Dad's hiding the booze."

"I knew it was a mistake to buy Michelangelo that painting set!"

"He says will you be his rôle-model?"

"I don't know why you want a new baby when I'm not even broken yet..."

"But darling, lots of children start walking at fourteen months!"

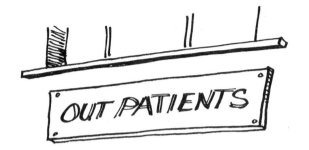

"NO, YOU CAN'T KEEP IT — THROW IT BACK WHERE YOU GOT IT FROM!"

"I think we're over the worst!
Our boy's out of Transcendental
Meditation and into
accountancy!"

"MUM! IT'S THE MAN WITH THE WALL-TO-WALL INSOLE!"

"HE AGREED TO PLAY WITH THEM BUT HE DIDN'T KNOW THE KITCHEN WAS OVERRUN WITH ANTS!"

HE'S A TREE DOCTOR ...

"I've been given seventy years to live."

93

"I don't mind going to Sunday School, it means I can sin like mad the rest of the week."

"This is what Dad calls Mom's maintenance and repair area."

"Happy Mother's Day!"

"Stop telling everyone that I'm always behind bars – I'm a barmaid!"

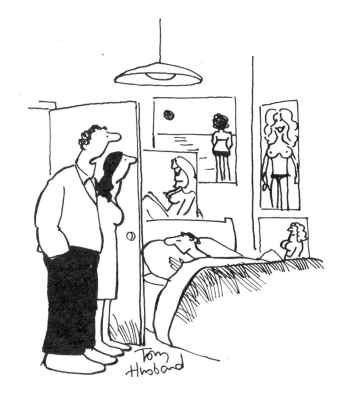

"I used to have team photos of Manchester United on my wall."

98

"For heavens sake, can't you stop asking me what I want to be when I grow up?"

"What about *my* side of the story?! Force-fed with sprouts and still made to wear flares!"

"I've got my school report Dad – you didn't do very well."

" I SUPPOSE IT'LL BE THE SAME AGAIN TONIGHT — WAKING UP AND ASKING FOR WATER ! "

"The sooner you're discovered the better –
you are costing me and your dad a
fortune in electricity . . ."

"We better turn it down a bit –
Dad's trying to do my homework."

"My elder brother's upbringing was according to Spock.
But mine's been more influenced by Milton Friedman."

"You didn't mention anything about waking Daddy up first."

"No thanks – not whilst I'm driving!"

HE'S QUITE BRIGHT — SO WE'VE BEEN ADVISED TO TAKE AWAY HIS GLASSES IN CASE HE GETS AN UNFAIR ADVANTAGE

"I've got an identity crisis, Dad. You were a Teddy Boy. My uncles were Hell's Angels. My cousins were Hippies. My brother is a Skinhead. My sister is a Punk and there's just nothing original left to be."

"What's in this? – Just in case
I'm rushed to hospital!"

"OH DO BE QUIET, AUDREY AND LET HIM
PLAY WITH YOUR DOLL FOR ONCE ! "

"Actually it's not about the birds and bees Son – it's about ammeters, electric shocks and transplants!"

1

"I've decided to give you both another chance."

"He's not so tough really – when Mum borrows the credit card he breaks into tears."

BIG TOP

113

"Look, John, would you mind if I reverted to calling you 'Dad'? I'm going through an identity crisis."

114

"That wasn't what you called him last night Dad!"

"Mine look intelligent too – but actually they're both useless at trigonometry."

"I know how you feel about corporal punishment but sometimes I wish you'd just whack him with it!"

"I suppose you know you're wrecking the quality of our TV reception?"

"De-programme him
and pack him
off to bed."

118

"That's right Son, just gently slip the key under the door!"

"...And so like his father!"

"If your father doesn't throw me out soon – I might not be allowed to come again!"

" YOU WANT AN ELEPHANT ? WHAT'S WRONG WITH THE ONE YOU'VE ALREADY GOT ? "

" PHEW ! BABY PUT UP QUITE A FIGHT TONIGHT, DEAR ! "

"My parents only
like classical music . . .
y'know – Beatles,
Shadows, Stones . . ."

123

"He flatly refuses to go through
a rebellious phase."

"It's your own fault, you've been
too lenient with your parents."

125

"How can you communicate with someone who never watches the commercials!"

The publishers would like to thank the following cartoonists who kindly contributed their work.

Barry Appleby
Sally Artz
David Austin
Jim Barker
Les Barton
John F. Beauchamp (Butch)
Clive Collins
Manny Curtis
Pat Drennan
Tony Ellis
David Follows
Noel Ford
Patrick Gallaghar (Patrick)
Alex Graham
James Gubb (Naylor)
Mick Harper
Frank Holmes (Quanda)
Tony Husband
Anthony Hutchings

Chic Jacob (Chic)
David Langdon
Tim Madden
Peter Maddocks
Norman Mansbridge
G.K. Marriott (Grock)
P.J. McNeilly
David Myers
Terry Parkes (Larry)
Michael Peyton
Ken Pyne
A.F. Ralley (Rali)
W. Scully
Charles Sinclair (Chas)
Glyn Wall
Colin Wheeler
Kipper Williams
Tom Williams (Quentin)